T0151089

BOOKS BY ANSELM BERRINGAN

Some Notes on My Programming (Edge Books 2006)

Zero Star Hotel (Edge Books 2002)

Integrity & Dramatic Life (Edge Books 1999)

Co-editor, with Alice Notley and Edmund Berrigan,
The Collected Poems of Ted Berrigan (UC Press 2005)

FREE CELL

CITY LIGHTS SPOTLIGHT SERIES NO. 2

ANSELM BERRIGAN

FREE

CELL

CITY LIGHTS

SAN FRANCISCO

CITY LIGHTS SPOTLIGHT
The City Lights Spotlight Series was founded in 2009, and is
edited by Garrett Caples, with the assistance of Maia Ipp.

Library of Congress Cataloging-in-Publication Data
Berrigan, Anselm.
Free cell / Anselm Berrigan.
p. cm.
ISBN 978-0-87286-502-0
1. Experimental poetry, American. I. Title.
PS3602.E7635F74 2009
811'.6—dc22
2009023360

Cover image: Untitled [detail], 1991
By John Anderson, courtesy the Weinstein Gallery
http://www.weinstein.com/

The editor would like to thank Rod Smith, John Anderson, and Brittany
Storey (Weinstein Gallery) for their assistance with this book.

All City Lights Books are distributed by the trade by
Consortium Book Sales and Distribution: www.cbsd.com

For small press poetry titles by this author and others,
visit Small Press Distribution: www.spdbooks.com

City Lights Books are published at the City Lights Bookstore,
261 Columbus Avenue, San Francisco, CA 94133

www.citylights.com

For Karen

Acknowledgments

Versions of these poems have previously appeared in the following mags and journals, the editors of which are thanked mightily by the author: *The Poker, morning train, Jubilat*, Secondavenue.com, *Wig, Detroit Stories, Tool*: A Magazine (online), *P.F.S. Post* (online), *Konundrum Engine Literary Review, Boog News*, mipoesias.com, *Verse, Phoebe*, and *They Were Flying Planes*.

Grateful thanks to Cy Press for publishing "Have A Good One," and to Letter Machine Editions for publishing a version of "To Hell With Sleep." Thanks also to the Composers Collaborative for commissioning a piece between the author and composer David First that turned into "Let Us Sample Protection Together." Thanks to Hald Hovedgaard in Denmark for hosting the Danish-American Writers' Retreat in 2007, during which time much of "Have A Good One" was worked out.

Anselm Berrigan is primarily published by Edge Books, an independent publisher of poetry and poetics founded by Rod Smith and based in Washington, D.C. The first issue of Smith's magazine *Aerial* appeared in 1984. Edge Books began publication in 1989. For more information, please visit http://www.aerialedge.com/edgebooks.htm.

CONTENTS

HAVE A GOOD ONE

Have a Good One

Not bellowing for mercy.

Not arming the donkeys.

Have a Good One

The compatibility of cynicism
and conviction would unnerve
my foundations were I not
conjoined with friendship
itself at its staggering wake. I
looked up and saw business
associates all around. I'd only

risen too quickly before faces
set back in. But the gestures
in mind, the icing of all personal
bureaucracies seemed done.
References, references in the deep.

Have a Good One

I didn't come writing

out of the womb

you know.

Have a Good One

You are

what your

record says

you are

Have a Good One

Maybe I can write all
poems I should have
written tonight this year.
Stupid lonely work ethic
driving me to puke ant wars
on two-star unusable patios.
Shan't be getting wrecked
or how long will I own
this porous be? A trick
gesture's enfeebled question.
Don't like covers. But getting
away from it all is beautiful
treason in the land of cheese
eating surrender monkeys. I
feel ugly and hairless. No, I

feel randy and beerless. The
flea-flicked play action as
part of the martial brain.
Lead by screams. I hereby
invent anonymous gods
to look out for the terminally
inhibited. Go forth, and bend
not these ugly fates toward
their piss-ant excuses for darkness.
Don't kill anyone I know.

Have a Good One

My mission tonight is to
not get so drunk I can't properly
emcee. It's surprisingly easy,
because I'm thinking about experience.

Have a Good One

Fathom cost by merit
of vainly wracked advances
to light takedown's mist.

Keeping under wrapped pace with
market forces' multi-orbital yet
self-revolving mis-circulation

of service's inference. You will
have more or less money at less
value in the near future. Ideas?

Have a Good One

Choose your own adventure
lacked possibility. Try
coming home to your
wildlife books sold off
by adult creep types
after enduring Boulder's
second grade. You're hopelessly

out of touch with the culture
you use by looking at. You
can be culture, but not
accused of it. Dream giant
cockroach in the wall
dreams, more often
pull endless string
from the mouth.

Have a Good One

history pops
noble usury, redemption
dusting off the rubble
for an unrated peek: cushy, etc.
resistance, etc.
existence threatened
indie section
on demand
street selling a future option:
handing out

poems like the free
cell guy.
That *300* unconsciously reflected
a culture losing its mind
is what I liked
about it.

Have a Good One

Non-identification has its rewards.
Hey dude. In the sightless ocean
deep, red-colored shrimp can't
see red. Other creatures that
emit red light dine well at
the expense of such weakness.

Have a Good One

Missed yr duration
while streaming
froth backwards
gazing to isolate
paunchable staid vitriolic
intimacy within
the just purely
not believable
destruction of Troy.
Nope. Now
I'm fusticating flarf
suppositories in my own
bought-into home.
But my truths
equate to
desert holes
secreted in absentia
tears. Mine. Boom.
It is like that
around me.
Ask the animals.
Senility managing
back page stability.

Tone Dead, I mean deaf
she calls me
with   joy.

"Unprofessional"
a punk from Hell calls me.

I should

do   research?

Have a Good One

It's a comfort to pine
for a drill sergeant.

Be eating out yourself
some time & smile at me

but don't come to me.
Impressive mind, not in skull.

Have a Good One

Schwag measures the night
meaning I've been through
the drawers of this stranger's house
& found the path
to mild depravity.

Have I not walked it before
by anyone's standards?
Anyone's high
non-exclusionary
standards?

Have a Good One

Stop telling me
I look tired.

I know what
I look like.

Tell me
how I feel.

Have a Good One

When they kill us
they'll find us
        attracted to their
            forms

followed by
a new Man Vs.
        Wild

Have a Good One

Chilled crap garage.
For my part its
been an honor
to be at someone's
service, though doing
so has diminished
my expiration date
and my astral self-
projection has already
fled in bitter tears
having used up even
addiction. But my
physical self really
gets politics, baseball
and the art of listening.
And I still have friends.
More, even.

I think you should win

Have a Good One

I've been punished into caring

about how it all shakes out for
us too. Resentment does drive

me into the arms of that or who
I resist, momentarily. I will

drink your father's wine & move on
You won't care. A thank you note

may will itself your way in some
store-bought form. Make me

stop telling the form to rethink
its life. Pleather clouds beckon

to us assassins. That's your
whole fucking work, enemy.

I don't name animals.
I don't steal their forms.
Barbarian camps circa 235
A.D. are hardly worthy of
condemnation fifteen hundred
years later. Goodbye health
plan. Goodbye semi-motivated
halflife of an identity.

It's no small amount
of information, the history
of food production. My name

is soft eerie music. There's
a they for you
out there   "There
is?"

There

is.

Have a Good One

17 watching Simon's apartment
summer of '90; bought acid
at Washington Square Park

to peak under Times Square lights.
Would all be very different
now had the shit been real.

Have a Good One

frydom's
sublime
heresy:
to fight
to have
nothing
said of
significance
and win
daily an
archaic
wing of
lament

Have a Good One

Tell it what it is.

Have a Good One

16

Finally, I'm okay with spiders.
I'd like an ugly president. I just
smashed a creature. I quit drinking
and lost eight pounds. I think
many formally expressed ideas
sound familiar. I discovered
recently that God's death was
the Big Bang. I'm half of being
halfway through a pregnancy. I'm
not speaking enough with family.
I'm leaning towards the avant-garde
as quaint. I broke my resolution.
I'm broaching the limits of not
driving's integrity. I'm losing more
vision in the right eye. I remembered
firing a semi-automatic rifle as a pre-teen
this past summer. I'm being pestered
by some fly. I'm happy within working.
I'm unable to answer most e-mail.

Have a Good One

Explanation befits a mirrored
version of me, so I
move on.

Have a Good One

Burying the duck
crumble with beer
while it pretends
to the elucidation
of principles.
The shaver sucks
face. Scotch shirt
proudly wrinkled.
Parisian sidewalk stains
& their lack of warmth.
Remember lava flowing
freely all around us
stains with warmth?
I've had a great life.
But I ain't going

out like that.

Have A Good God One

Back to the drawn board
you'll make me shoot.

Everything will be alright.

Have A Good One

Prissy cops
take stands

on blurb distribution:
the opening of a new

reading season. Mutually
assured non-embarrassment.

Don't slice the pooks
contrapunktus.

Have A Good One

Onset buckaroo voyeurstan
following moons around.
Woe to stacks.

Miss them severed heads
taking spare change
I do not.

Have A Good One

pay the date to remember you
enemy of salience

history's meet & greet

calls upon your caption

Have A Good One

I was distant because
        I mistrust my face

        I was distant because I
                didn't want to engage your interruption

                I wasn't distant, but I was
                        preparing for an onslaught

I have incorporated new strategies
        into approaching large, active
                somewhat known crowds
                        & I was mulling over the possibilities

        I drank some coffee & was trying
                to remember the bathroom's location
                        & get there

Blame it on biology, psychology
    self-consciousness, familiarity
amiable dread, calculation and
        general contentedness

Have A Good One

    only through porous antique
      gestures of will can our love
        be truly maintained as the set
    of administrative functions we
require it to be, so as to weave
    and burn with philanthropic glee

Have A Good One

Fuck radar?
Cringeability –
a last function

in service of public
meltups: the
world's its own
example, & I'm
co-bringing life
into it. *High* cringe
factor, for the feint
of heart. "Have a
good baby."

Have A Good One

O organ dicing double down

O enemies' bugged psyches

Have A Good One

Flock of ass kickers
in sight of paranormal
disability. Pixel kid's
chicken bone on cold
Cardinal game night
dreams internet into
owned consciousness:
nations of antibodies
protecting egg at planet's
core from capillary
aardvark skill balloons.
Never has my symbiote
been so disturbed as to
believe cliché a sign of
desperation in the cheery
rainy real fireworks of a
new boss. What was —
happy birthday Mom —
the deciding factor?
I'm shaken, utterly
by the kindly ones
having killed Dream.

Have A Good One

Who would you like
to have make the big
decisions for you?

Have A Good One

Waving goodbye
to an era of
impersonal
accumulation
I mean, waving
goodbye to instant
reflection disguised
as something in
charge, moths
dive-bombing
lights.

Have A Good One

It's been good to
celebrate impure
origins. I'll pros-
titute this ability
to celebrate for
awhile longer
I like to think.
Or viciously snap
to attention, when
the moment
strikes, an imprint
of spontaneity.
Slutty chimney,
teleporting
ruthlessly
to the middle.
I'm all I'm
comfortable
with lately.

Have a Good One

Paid loan payment before

sending masters on

their way. Time

you ruinous agent of

possibility, will you ever

truly get your point across?

Or unfreeze & send back

more to the point

all them corrosive

explanations of yr work?

Monolithic derelict fuck.

Have A Good One

Give me your taxable
contours. The caveman
did. The rain in stride
zoned us to passable
educations reflective
after a time. Our guts
for once don't make
a break for it. Their
deadly attacks merely
entertain inside upon
request: nature feigns
oversight. I'll break
the law for an exo-
skeleton panelist of
woe. Give it back.

Have A Good One

"The choices your work

left me were to submit

or walk out

& you have not

earned my submission."

Have A Good One

It's become harder and harder
not to take responsibility. For
all of it. Every bastion of
disrepair, every qualified public
apology for ill-tongued remarks.
Every pasture of redespair, every

made up résumé of a sorry. Its
been harder not to undergo surgery
or plead for indifference from the
feds. Don't you see them seeing you?
Remember when them seeing us was
what we wanted? And yet I was in
high school: The President's Daddy
was the President.

Have A Good One

Production values
among other grandchildren
of Mallarmé

spilling frozen
chicken thighs
all over the tracks

Have A Good One

On the birthday hunt

'tis quaint

is it not

to kill for peace

to saw through bone

as sample

of surgical

precision

to throw a ball

around with

your fellow prisoners?

Have A Good One

In the error
    thinking of non-intervention
        with you. A red sun
            (don't look) pokes
        through. Staging
    development and the cutting
loose of its facile integrity
    its disproportionate
            personal non-response.
        The wince. The shrug. The
            belated semi-acknowledgment
                of owning just
                    enough to take part.
        In the era, thinking of you
            will quit my job
                in one year to get
            more done, work harder
                to insert myself into
            the fragile extension
        of space between us

to get something done.
In the ear
thinking after you.

Have A Good One

A vow's form
like hills echo-ed

that cheer we may
succumb to shortly

Have a Good One

We refused to enter Tompkins
Square Park by 1986
though we were always told
by the grumpier neighbors
who thought our wiffle balls

would break their windows
the park was where we were
supposed to be. The park wasn't
for us, and we knew that. And
you couldn't play wiffle ball
in the park – you needed stories
to hit against. We didn't mind
that the park was fucked up
but we weren't going there.
Then those neighbors made
us move up to the corner of
St. Mark's Place and First Ave.
The site was okay, but all
these dealers appeared
wanting to get just one
swing, which of course
turned into a million.

Have A Good One

Off the record
he's a piece of shit.
Time management
I don't buy.
Just tell me
what's happened.
Whatever it's
going to be
is what
I need
to know.

Have a Good One

theme: I am supposed to be asleep

ordered to chair tractable

downy platitudes

smoked some resin before landing

velvet nodding pony nodding

strafe jingle soothes momentary hex

sinking be the ship

the scholastic revelation paradox

while quietly bludgeoning when I want

a strand of painterly disaffection.

The mind arrives

with inept wonder

imitating trumpets

or some shit that's thoroughly

made the transition   from court to commercial.

What are you defending

if the use of the right

is in question? So

deeply ingrained

as to be gone. Watched

it go. But we're still here

and I'm handing you this gun

you're already holding

Have A Good One

It's hard
to be
a good
boy. Harder
than being

magick. I
think I
look better
when I
don't shower.

Have A Good One

Birdy shoots out from treetop

swallows pen

laid down

leave them bugs alone boy

sleep — dream back to

yourself — the you you

remember yourself to be

when I sleep   sleep takes

less from me than

I need

I belong anywhere

as if to belong

no particular place

there's a city of

strangers for me despite

my predilections

mind invents & retrieves faces

when I shut my eyes

the chest has been

weakened by my own hand

am on a farm

    writing   eyes closed

     back to grass

I don't aim to kill

    anything but will

     take responsibility

      for thousands upon

    billions of deaths if

       all these bugs stop

        crawling on me

Have A Good One

So what
    that you're
independent.
    Everyone here
is independent.
    That's why we
can be nukers.

Call me down
    but don't play
it like you're
    so free
it doesn't matter
    how thoroughly
you've humiliated me

Have a Good One

Snorting this slowly
growing spinal fluid
sno-cone is fucking
with my mind: must
not let details get in
the way of principles.
Or was that the other
way around? Volume

considered adjusted.
Every single formal
structure advanced
by thieves.

Have A Good One

If today is the day
of the plunged

pliable if

may I speak

from the resourceful

catastrophe
of our basic

public services
& cry tears of relief?

Have a Good One

They went for it is not
the droid I'm looking to

for convivial disengagement
from soul. For that I've come

to your cadaver's waltz
of a special place for

lonely childhoods. I wasn't
lonely until just now, love

all around like an historical
landmark. They'll be

expensive, those original specs.
That rusted gate has to meet

its own dignitay. Get
as they say, your own.

Loneliness will merely gnaw
at our vocabulary.

Have A Good One

Stomp a sure fire crowd
a chilled echo directed.
Expectorate a prudentially
divisive phaser withnail
leaving the merely rich
behinds. I hate progressives
and their inexorable drive
toward emphasis. Let
someone kill someone.

Have A Good One

May I be broken open
to lead the walk

Am qualified as a relativity.
The abyss more fellow stranger
than invocation made by lover
of questionable judgment. I checked
out sunken treasure in a deep public freeze
today. The hieroglyphic tax records were beauteous.
Don't sanction the general pity bodiless foot with base
nor disentangle my anonymity from your well-funded scuba
research & palatial underwater soundtrack. Stuck to the planet's
limits, via obsessed demon-heart revival or storied advance
of constant reinvention, I'm not preserving the integrity of the
republic no more. I don't need masthead succor from every
human angle. Withdrawal is my own minor accomplice
at heart. Seizure. Tyranny. Be mine all to myself.

Have A Good One

I can't help.

I'd use an army
of Thucydides clones.
They'd record the entirety
of pleas for assistance
exchanged by sackable cities.
Beat them. Over their heads.

Have A Good One

I'm on my own side now
posting fee, a relative
quilt, a dish to Yao
under the bucket,
a nudge to will us
into being our own advocate
in the ER. This business
of being pushy to get
care has to happen
but the residents flee
when they see me
coming. You can't judge

the heat. May your
qualifications for
treatment sing beside
your bed, patient 23.
Meowers turn inside out.

Have A Good One

The problem with free will
is not that it does or does not
exist, but that it's pointless.

Have A Good One

Pint balanced on beak.
Pre-emptive fluff
in quality trash sync
with gentrified protest
against the sweet song

of cronyism. No.
O acid blood
demystified
in the meta-squall
aquiver. Poly-flammable
apparitions and calibrated
scuzz for sale.
They, comrade
spite the bitten neck
for throbbing so wound-like.

Have A Good One

a fundamentally sound clubhouse cancer

I got caught up
in the memorial biz
I let people let me
hurt their feelings

Have A Good One

Let's step out of the day

    for an unscripted haunting

across time   I sharpen   my teeth

        needing boats
        to exterminate

the wooly rhino
    & fuck yr flock

     afore ye knew

  a need to possess

     cargo

I have imagined saying no so often and rarely ever fantasize a yes.
One may own a strategy what contains spitting yes repeatedly as

a tactic leading to the fulfillment of a grand vision that will be the
unmistakable embodiment and subsequent catatonic astral eruption
of a no.

             my kissable lifeline
                  illustrates foraging
             via $20 burgers
                                      silence in public
                                      is how I work
                  wonder of mortality
                       & risk being tarred elegiac
             some risk   & if I can't wait to properly age, hon?

by dusk
    by yard
by splintered coalition
    by foot
        by guided missile
        by gathered mind's porous non-fear of shit like owning a house
            by delicate flower
                by aphoristic glee of doom in the proto-fauna
                    by being prone to negotiate
                by need for a new sack

by not wanting to argue every god damn day
    by artificial pond
  by blunders rung up to get beat down
by ecstasy of refusal
      by right's side dull discomfort growing daily
    by above all's fierce intellect

I'll summon resistance gets used a lot by academics these days. Get rewarded by a monkey fucking a football or spin the chore sheet, and these things have character and what is that character, how can I convey it or channel it into an intro? I will give my sister-in-law a book about modernism for Chanukah, and my mother something to steal from. To a colleague in the upper American north wilds perhaps an explanation of the difference between ghosts and subject matter. Some perjury for the comrades, and a lovely pink slip for moi.

Have A Good One

The promise of a hard-won exuberance
brought you near. The need to be

around the most people doing
something was a fucking magnet. From
           running races to making copies to
           delivering packages promotion became
           a recognizable cycle, if always
           with a clear ceiling or escape hatch.
           The latter you design, though awareness
           of authority in that regard can be
           transient. It's a cheap shot. Honesty
           in the making. But do the parts get to
           be themselves while part of the whole
           thing? And if they're only themselves
           like I'm only my habits and kindnesses
           measuring contact before moving
           forward we're done. You'll call me.
           I tend to screen. Technology's
           beauty made shapely by the choice.
           Bits of it, I mean. Shape is for the birds.

                              Have A Good One

Let us celebrate death
with a magnificence
worthy of the reader.

Have A Good One

"There exists in human nature a strong
propensity to depreciate the advantages &
to magnify the evils of present times."   —Edward Gibbon

Dear Queen
don't look at me
from yr in-flight
back of seat
entertainment screen
You can stick a finger
breaded if you prefer
into the asshole of empire
and hope for implosion
but you're just as likely
to get it off. That's my

idea of didactic poetry
by the way. One faceless
decision after another
idea wars waged without
curiosity.

Have A Good One

swaggery bro store
in my change purse
a scream across
an airshaft
a polite return
of stolen organs
when one awakens
I contain
a toxic avenger
will unleash her
as an unspeakable trance
to order time
to bend furtively

that which cannot
get to its
innate thatness.

Have A Good One

Don't mind seeming
like I might
if pushed

Have A Good One

Twinge interrupted
massive bumblebee fear.
But it don't notice me.
Back to padded
backpack, leaning
up against
a Danish tree.

Have A Good One

I need to be near
temptation in order
to avoid it. It feels
good to turn down
drinks by paying for
their company. They
just sit by my paper.
Jewels inside animals
begun as masking agents.
I like the way this bug
is walking up the finger.
Or we, the convivial
trainwreck, like it.

Have A Good One

My problem
with perception

can't shake
the feeling

it's less than
targeted.

Three planes
nothing

depends upon
fly by

Have A Good One

Everyone here paints themselves
red and devours monkeys – there's
an abundant supply. I, on
the other hand, a hooker with
a heart of gold, will no longer
get paid to make arrangements,
i.e., the art's on its own.

Have A Good One

Innumerable frites

squatting oh so near.
I need some polytheists
in my life, or an undead
Captain America. I
wouldn't mind coming
near the candidates
as keyboard solos. Partially
unemployed, with child
momentarily.

Have A Good One

I get stoned to pay

my bills, make modifications

to the alcove. Reverse momentum:

a red rocking chair rides fault lines

over every dime I've made. Being

picked up by a hawk is no cure.

Have A Good One

What I know is
    the birds sing back

Have A Good One

Mousey in the parrot's
    sleeping bag
    now faced me.
    Perchance the
       pock-eyed squeaker
    might perform

                                        a suddenly necessitated
                                               by birth
                                             laproscopy?

Have A Good One

I'm currently in the hosting
business. A guy comes through
using his quasi-imminent death
as a trading chip for time and
space to do his thing. Advises
me to make enemies. Week 183
out of 204 on the clock. He shows
his slides. He nips a flask. He reads
and doesn't die. One week later
he's behind the reception table
after someone else's reading.
"I've always thought of you
as my ersatz-son," he tells me.

Have A Good One

The History Channel
on Planet of the Apes

Have A Good One

Twiddling identities
while babies and bombs
go unclaimed. I'm looking
around the symphony
crowd for my type:
elastic, fresh, deceased,
loaded, "engaged,"
with experience at
the front. If you're
too busy for the five
billion, I'm right for me.

Rust-colored water from
gurgling pipes, the eminence
gratis of mon canard, Sulla
p-proaching the city gates
again, this pisser
of a day's sylvan
lining: quit booze
for fuzzy water, easing in
chloroform love
writing off
the desire to be liberated

Have A Good One

Smaller bubbles and feisty
prognostication, but what
do the lasers mean
extinct sub-species?

When you slow down
time, work is not really
there, at the base of things
with this futile compulsion
to finish, implying that
resolve is useful while
surrendering potential.
Sound wants to thank.

Have A Good One

Must we demand
of our pop tarts
a public crack-up
during war time?

Can't we just give them
complimentary memberships
with the species
for eternity's duration?

Have A Good One

Six bulls in double figures.
        Genial solutions for those
    victimized by their private protoplasmic
                    quartet-like reasoned with
                ineffable hellish quality
                    pre-thoughts. Ask
                    the clams
                swirling round
            Jesus' tomb.

Have A Good One

                    In defense of self-awareness
                    I'd just say anger possesses
                    its own intelligence, subject
                    of course, to cherry-picking
                    or, at minimum, cherry-like
                    flavor. & if, like, calculations

get fleshed into the green room
as a consequence of my refusal
to keep filling slots, there'll still
be an incorporated body to
behold. I talk more and more
when a pure chance comes by.

Have A Good One

I do take relentless
as a compliment. All this work
dealing with making it work.
Pigeons own the top
of our a/c and I wonder
if we're breathing in
their shit. It's fall.
Someone quit something & I
can have it.
Am I supposed to keep
the blunt, arty
bafflement of cause

the job comes with?
I don't want you to come
and expect to stay.
I don't want to raise
a kid like me.

Have A Good One

It's like when
you need to be
owner and coach
is what I'm
talking about.
It's no use
being torn in
five to twelve
pieces. There's
no manual, no
ethical sub-routines
to delete. Scary
to ride a jet-propelled

shopping cart off
some pithy lake
pond middle class
dock. "Any loss
of life is tragic,"
a spokesperson
added.

Have A Good One

Kingfisher sighting sparks
epic stroll. Dollerup Hills
touch moors & keep me out
of mind a little longer. The
impossibility of being true
does not divine any future
moves here, a vacant comfort
a developing relationship
with the shapes of horror.
Job in makeup: well, no
I'm not terribly qualified.

Back to the brink, as ever.

Have A Good One

I was taunted by
a sheep and her
lamb today, in
a Jutland field.
They roam free
here, and I was
failing to make
a call or the phone
was failing. The
two stood parallel
to one another
staring at me while
I strolled by. They
rotated in silence
to continue staring
as I continued
strolling and

gradually vanished
from view.

Have A Good One

Just wasted
and taking it.
In life
I rally
constantly.
Effort is what we
breach. And
accountability.
Honed limits
do you require
ruthlessness or subtlety?
The # for that delivery service
I could find. My
instinct is to agree
with the collective.
I'll flip over

their indoor/outdoor
reversible rug.
But my feelings
& their representatives
the passing sacrosanct
mob cuddle
stirring expedience
are mine. Gradations
of default tenor.
Anything but more instinct.
A proxy of determination
in a cosmic discharge salon
speaking freely of cost's
elephantine deployable
former charm.
I'm micromanaging nausea.
The dishes are twilighting.
The dairy scythe elevatrix
skins my shining
teleprompted sporkdom.
As poor specimens
go, the trail left
inhabitable trails.

Arkanoid as meditative
space, if we travel by
dragonfly. I cling
to thy moving perimeter.
I want payment
for all instances
of being caught
on camera. We
all should.
Mutually
assured destruction
overdosed on civility
by comparison.
Babywiping lead paint
dust from my soles.
I'll read entrails
for omens, action
figure entrails.

Have A Good One

The expression of a speck
of life, impractically speaking
is gonna make it hard to walk

Have A Good One

When I am withdrawn
& avoid eye contact
but show up to the doctor place

carry the bag
clean up the mouse shit
pick up the order, the boxes
nod at the general purpose
& don't speak
on those days
it's in order to do
the things I have to do
and not sink
into ownership

of my present as built
habit by habit
deception by deception

Have A Good One

Your voice dear
kicking in and out
by entrance to
an old oak forest
—a small parcel of
decidedly non-agg-
ressive trees—gives
me assurance. I
want constantly
not to know
what's going to
happen, in order
or under orders
to be surprised.
What's it training

for? A hopeful
sense of stage, a
confidence out of
mind to bring up
a kid who could be
our friend. The exchange
is one tiny opening
among countless
openings we work
with, working for.

Have A Good One

let me
swim in
the grease
I love

Have A Good One

Yes

LET US SAMPLE PROTECTION TOGETHER

When I was little I cut off the heads
of many lords. I can't count on the energy
that took to rise in me at will, but I've
strengthened my ability to make a
stand-firm surface. A steady gaze will drive
conflicted information away, back to the
abyss from whence it came, but I'll be right
here the morning after, wracked in a
private shame too awful to admit and
of no consequence at all. I work very hard
not to let myself go. Any channel
can tell. Due process appears in beauty
and misgiving at once; an agility
borne from creative malice, a benign
insecurity. The plain truth: I forget
the curtains are open sometimes and the
hands wander. The room stares back from its things:
They understand the end of the world, will
not waste time feeling your pain, and every-
thing tragic in between need not be known.

I don't want love or remorse to follow
I want them in the way, things to burst through
corollaries to be roped and tackled
by surprise, get killed, and thank you. One fate
transforms into another, but I won't
touch that bandaged story. I won't belong
to this scripted conversation, though I
may play along. Identity theft accepting
renewal orders, copycat pre-emptive attacks
an obscure murder string on the public
glide by sight, the victim a John doughnut
pining for leadership from the passenger seat.
The threat of meaning reassures: I know
it's being made for me. Am I supposed
to believe we're receiving information?
Can I defect back to curiosity
in the moonlight, stone rabbit? Hit on by
Echo, I go cold for the love of my
own exile, and while I hope, my flesh
explodes into an arrangement of stars
pestered by darkness. Those aren't birds you
hear, just their corresponding holes in the sky.
All the bottled water isn't fooling anyone.

TO HELL WITH SLEEP

Leave a pretty cop, go forth

Leave a pretty cop, go forth
animated voice machinations
aslop, in relation to enemy
tacit replaces fucking, grim
pink stripes, fleeced okapi
snowsuits bloggering credenzas
parsed whales come hither.

No objects soothe, sculptural
collar, socks as eggs, get
fresh, should na done, part
drawn as she-wolf, mauve
fangs, well, pobresito, every

body treat you so mean, pat
pat pat in the cage jersey cage

strapped for foptropy, in
the down search mines, I's
driving greens to save, to
staunch a union pucker
winsome, further, making it
few. Vowel flame sicced to
constant bind, I dunno my

owned impression, there gives
no, study of thinking, horse-
man, horse-headed-man, stays
an order, runs a program
a hedge against protection
but scratch, non-choice, I
've intangibles, I, fucking, win.

Motrin lotion anti-fungal
pigeon love forever, no
spikes decorate this landing
to conserve your energy

screaming stickless lite
bulb, 5th century A.D.
treaty lusts for labor, bacon

wit every ping – why did
I let that kid in my class?
Why did I inhale upside-
downed margaritas? Why
did I wear the "Free Bob
Perelman" sticker? Why
attend shadow inaugural?

Who has a right to my
oath? Why when you ain't
looking? You don't, bro
get the croc back, late era
smoochy on the micro-
cellular leveler, a humor
turns to interrogate some

take out's tonal pageantry
radical transportation
muting conceptually rich

spunk, grit, x-factor
hustle, John Candy's hair
clumps in Stripes, every
last as if it's my game.

In a box in a box in a

In a box in a box in a
ring, a seconds few
casualty free for a
co-memorative tumble
a mirage consistency
gots amiable pressure
from, deer say, weck

memories unworthy of
a debonair elusivity, a
gold star's robot spine.
I am not so reliant on
toughing out a respectable

lie – what I hide hides, a
shared joy with strangers

you know, the movies, like
that, spigot love, between
corneous faith waves, fingered
radioactively, pieced together
determined neutral, reso-
lution surface bloviates
musters waste for a drop of

silence. Now I come to avoiding
daylight's reedy taxations with
you, neon beside contractions
in the artificial vim of
alphabet city, a pleasure
to sense, carnival alarm
triggers nursing at a once

certain now dictated
time, to be a panic, a
history of connection so
felt as to be vulgar, in

formal obsession, not live
for what will never be, a
dear question, an anything.

Yeah, I screamed in my
  child's ear, but not at
    her, her formation, just
      just my own pulse-ridden
        fam flex o'er cheer's
          vacated drain; once I dug
            to be tackled in my, my

              own drizzle-friendly street
              repeating meals from inept
              hands, a wonder to pause for
              between the usual sacrilegious
              kindnesses of our tribe, the
              gourmand's feathery tones
left out for a little hunted

peck, I'm groovy, where go?
  Fat collected shame of a
    onesy, one gets that

nothing's there if made
to vote, by appearance of
yeah, for now, mesh digs
me, half a chair, pooky.

On hands & knees singing

On hands & knees singing
for water to be owned
robbing glee to pay hey
Paul, hey plotz let's be
the head-2-head shoot-
out honey inserts to be-

friend autonomy shops.

Single changeling face
place, spry chlorine-free
rashish, the considerable
sycophant's amnio-add-

iction trampolines, in-
guinal folds trek to mess-
age: I don't care

where you've been as
long as it was deep
torturing debaser rhythms
to be other worlds, ones
we understand as ones to
sing Miss Piggy, sing with
Kris Krissy, & fear no empty

life's hoary tremulous well
maybe scratch throated
lullaby inversions to wake
the disengaged who hold
the so-called power one
senses outside of our
chaste flame of seething

something more inviting
a permanent refuge for
the transient as consigned

bluster klutz, elegant demi-
hillbilly non-accentual
urban nerds perfecting
an awkward care with

unconscious rigor. Do
you get your derivation
high? Does its daddy
cry? Let in moneybags'
electorate for a long-
awaited birthday of
raw thrills, tempted

monkeys in heaven, they
own me, not you, not
your perfect minded
devotion to an intimate
fall; ratcheted frame
may save money with a
co-signer, but the light

too's deactivated there.
As image transmission

names itself more direct
— you can see the cracks
in some hockey player's
teeth mid-check — we go
on with unregistered bliss.

Breathing seizes shapes

Breathing seizes shapes
of a blast, asleep, awaggle
for the plain dramatics
stricken by new life, fans
taser the heart of a feckless
underdog's triumph as
we script its mock return

but who's asking for a red-
lipped star-spackled clam
tilted on its side to befriend
a kid free of language? As

reportage machetes its own
split infinity, or switch
blades its hunters' breakfast

or butter knifes any advance
from telegraphed duality
we outflank its metaporpoise
and drool back to selected
identities, agencies of bruise.
Kettle chips vanish, seed
all over the floor, ravenous

service. Tiny person duels
my temper, its ability to
shatter a selfish calm
we meet variously forced
back by routine into
the sum of my decisions.
This one's only for mien.

Looking around to describe
things by entry, book satchel
left on interstate by an

electronic name I now
meet after seven years, what
we do he asks & yap is
what we, bad brains, do.

This isn't a from I can
follow to a brink. I
want to let go of my
sense of destined socket
love taped to pre-season
bathysphere blues' goth
doctorate structures of

party time. All these heads
avail themselves for entry
for blighted starry recognition
for the gas of making it in
the critical tradition: I
want a five-dollar entry ethic
& in if you want and have

none. Airlifted dreams run
on misplaced verve a.k.a.

relief the new creature's
asleep and temporarily
unable to block your
petty advance with pure
need. No smiles yet pop.

I go many places, wakka

I go many places, wakka
wakka wakka, unscrew
many faces, wakka wakka
wakka, tears for the coffin's
delivery to barracks, the tea-
cher thrown out the win-
dow, out of state, her son's

music calms our space, more
feed, more pain, more growth.
A single non-blip of financial
scratch, unrecognizable her

digitized face, love in a
firefly's debauched wing
a NY Post of the jowl.

I'm glad for waste, its
ascension, its emotional arc
into the prose of governance.
Dumb hostilities issue forth
from all the movements of yester-
morrow: am I liberal when it
comes to prostitution? No.

Scores don't settle, all are
underpaid, one argues in
mind, let me go out of.
Fuckface's tipsy late, shall
we go back to chucking
the republic's enemies
from hill-tops, galactic pot?

Trying to be tender, salted
pork, the caring dirtbag
overqualified to swim

back into the job blitz
a kind guy who can give
orders, enemy of Bush &
Rimbaud, enemy of fate.

I am a laser, hold doors
open. Only. Only. Only.
She'll take your heart
but you won't feel it
maintain an unsteady
allegiance to gaps
in continuity. Its.

Cradle cap. Everything a
little much to absorb
no insta-chatter or happy
titan face. The wrong god
ate his kids, which meant
hiding them from himself.
Rivers get it done - non-

emblematic – in the
playoffs, enter Young.

Artificial reef bill to
zap commercials, the
outdoor beat declareth
getting rid of yr dollars
be the scary Pacific Rim.

Frailty puckers up to present

Frailty puckers up to present
gibberish in the agri-fab
spamways, helicopter can't
swim, can't junk tribal
penance for living off natty
whims so many pairs of
pants deny in fever's dash.

The routine bites hard, ooze
a rapt factory heir teething
sway, ye olde time cleaners
spun off a granted project

of abeyance in the deep
trim that art savors, bent-
like, creaming dabbles.

I had no models' friars
for the last long effort to
velvetize consciousness
& I been so long in a
keister-fixed dale I can't
see past the courtsy for
the corsage, nor represent

bubbly ethics dweamin' gills
for the unreversible future
like I love dust, I love little
anklet crumbies in my
zonk stricken dumbs, I
lithe serious plutos left
with snipped outer cheer.

Plural frag blue doven
a comfort case spiked
to divest screwtopic

champignon in pro-
sers' jacked up scurvy
wall-dag bakesale of
deep trans(con)scription.

Stinky cauterizes mountains
for kicks while I, I leak
state secrets in a dork
shark's archived
chomp and she, she
leans in for the sign:
angels and martians.

Tracking thing to be's
hapless improv roast
without embarrassed
dreams, perfect posture
rot, tufa-thwacked finger
picking to turn, friend.
That blare means to take

poise from my haid
skewered out of pitch.

The bomb drafts steam
reform, soothes mech-
anized appendage use.
I stay in bitty sight.
To hell with sleep.

Warble, easily smile

Warble, easily smile
howl an unfed energy
to howl, every record a
gallery, a touch of
body from, an ounce
of detection forming
total consensus awareness.

Hooky, pre-cancerous
appeal, wittle bomby
sampling the cowbell
when danger's character

was understood; when
zombies lose their appe-
tites can we rehabilitate

'em back into the game?
I sympathize with the
difficult people, why
should transitions be
seamless, Sylvie hates to
go to sleep, no she hates
the "go" part & so do I

awake, smiling toothlessly
at our anti-lyric non-concepts
our pro-war liberties, our
embrace of our own private
communiqués beseiged
for, like, happiness of
a minor place's kindling.

Out to no studio, I
can imagine being asked
questions, live trapped

miscellaneous camaraderies
to peddle not the ticket
but a gainful charismatic
seizure of blue enormity.

I was partying with sleep
made it grin, fleeced it
at some buddy hour
did I have to kill every-
thing in sight? Or just.
Liquify our symbols. Our
gluttonous ramifications.

Bounce bounce bounce
& a nun back in time gets
pissed. Bounce bounce the
booze ain't working. She'll
stand afore she rolls over, the
drool machine, and if it was
a test it would be graded.

Don't take the wheel
sleepyhead. Fussy a mode

of being, age ten days.
Ten Santas dived into the
Mars Bar mid-afternoon
one for each day. First
question: how to live.

Furtive or restive?

Furtive or restive?
Dibble or Knoblauch?
Ball-sniffing dog or
droolsultory ion cannon
sleep shots proofing
proofs? I like moving
your careful parts about.

I launch warrior
cavaliers into mama
dens' disaffected prayer
cycles. I sit alone in

my four-cornered room
staring at candles. Sunshield
or Purgatorio? Proto-cock-

eyed rhetoric or demonic
non-prosody on the shit
slant? The roaches did
everything together, & it
mattered. The roaches
swapped lovers & opinions
and metric affiliations.

I am currently only
lying to three-and-a-half
persons. Maybe nine.
Bracket special or post-
violence dearth machine?
Weak side help or heroic
annihilation? Deep Space

Nine or Jameson's neat?
Or. What would Kenny
Daniels think? What

would Dolphy or LeRoy
think? Or Molly Adams?
Or Bruce, outside, on
his knees, palms up, a

book on each hand?
Today I loathe less
than yesterday. I'm
waiting for the words
to come to me; it's
just a tactic, nary an end.
At the used frame shop

the cruel chase a world. Dan
Marino for Nutrisystem
tells good carbs from bad.
Jeanne, I do know her name
& it is Jeanne. Fucking brain's
insistence on its own sounds
its crush on ma'am. Call

Patrick or send message?
When does an old friend's

non-interest in eating
brains become a barrier
to friendship? Should I
invent an identity and
abuse its privileges?

Unknown knowns bind

Unknown knowns bind
me to history's fecund
splay of reform – old
friend writing through a
body to reach an 18th
century additive; plagiarized
body, coiling addiction.

Hairy fellas enter tile.
I don't but rarely feel
like I know anything
I'm that kind, everything

knowledge-wise a fight
but I get put in charge
often enough: beware.

Entering an adoration
from its emergency exit
one holds oneself well
picking up crumbs that fit
a vagrant niche in a
performance enhanced
exhibition of wild retro

gemless fine thin
actively exposed privacy.
What be all too clean.
Bear rattle, pocket king
rattle, up and in, refined.
Show me what I know
folds a dog ear back.

Vitrine policy scrunch.
Pristine viper summons.
Stammered painy ving.

Soundtrack memories.
The disenhanced O.
I bat a ladybug brain
hanged off ring. I hated

Rush, hated The Dead
Floyd, Zep. Hated bootlegs
& yr ugly monolithic stereo.
But today, the snuggle.
Phone log mind for rent.
I reframe myself. Whistle.
Dogma. Holy secular scumbag.

What's a lapel? What's
a threshold, precious?
I prefer aquadelegates.
I prefer them to still
be in the running for
America's Next Top
Model. Slowly I turned

toward the ornamentation
of a by-gone era, singing

of a guitarosaur's missing
 legs, a side order of carrion
  the arrogance of asking for
   aid, the body count's shadow
    work, a miniature transit.

ABOUT THE AUTHOR

Anselm Berrigan is a poet, identifies only as a poet, and works in service of that art while happy for the existence of all the others. *Free Cell* is his fourth full-length book of poems. Over the course of a decade, he served as volunteer, office assistant, reading series organizer, workshop leader, and, from 2003-2007, Artistic Director for the Poetry Project at St. Mark's Church in New York. He has taught composition and creative writing at a number of schools and independent literary organizations. He currently teaches at Pratt Institute and Wesleyan University, and co-chairs Writing at the Milton Avery Graduate School of the Arts, an interdisciplinary summer MFA program.

With his brother Edmund Berrigan and Alice Notley, he co-edited *The Collected Poems of Ted Berrigan*, which was published in 2005 by UC Press. He is a member of the subpress publishing collective, through which he has published books by poets Steve Carey and Hoa Nguyen. Currently Poetry Editor for *The Brooklyn Rail*, a monthly arts and culture newspaper (brooklynrail.org), he has received two grants from the Fund for Poetry, and a 2007 New York Foundation for the Arts poetry fellowship. Berrigan is married to poet Karen Weiser and the father of the recently-born Sylvie Berrigan.

The state of the world calls out for poetry
to save it. LAWRENCE FERLINGHETTI

CITY LIGHTS SPOTLIGHT SHINES A LIGHT ON THE WEALTH
OF INNOVATIVE AMERICAN POETRY BEING WRITTEN TODAY.
WE PUBLISH ACCOMPLISHED FIGURES KNOWN IN THE
POETRY COMMUNITY AS WELL AS YOUNG EMERGING POETS,
USING THE CULTURAL VISIBILITY OF CITY LIGHTS TO BRING
THEIR WORK TO A WIDER AUDIENCE. IN DOING SO, WE ALSO
HOPE TO DRAW ATTENTION TO THOSE SMALL PRESSES
PUBLISHING SUCH AUTHORS. WITH CITY LIGHTS SPOTLIGHT,
WE WILL MAINTAIN OUR STANDARD OF INNOVATION AND
INCLUSIVENESS BY PUBLISHING HIGHLY ORIGINAL POETRY
FROM ACCROSS THE CULTRUAL SPECTRUM, REFLECTING
OUR LONGSTANDING COMMITMENT TO THIS MOST
ANCIENT AND STUBBORNLY ENDURING FORM OF ART.

CITY LIGHTS SPOTLIGHT

1

Norma Cole, *Where Shadows Will:*
Selected Poems 1988-2008

2

Anselm Berrigan, *Free Cell*

3

Andrew Joron, *Trance Archive:*
New and Selected Poems

4

Cedar Sigo, *Stranger in Town*

5

Will Alexander, *Compression & Purity*

6

Micah Ballard, *Waifs and Strays*